THE FUNNIEST ENGLAND QUOTES... EVER!

Also available

The Funniest Liverpool Quotes... Ever!
The Funniest Chelsea Quotes... Ever!
The Funniest West Ham Quotes... Ever!
The Funniest Spurs Quotes... Ever!
The Funniest Arsenal Quotes... Ever!
The Funniest Man City Quotes... Ever!
The Funniest Newcastle Quotes... Ever!
The Funniest United Quotes... Ever!
The Funniest Leeds Quotes... Ever!
The Funniest Boro Quotes... Ever!
The Funniest Forest Quotes... Ever!
The Funniest Sunderland Quotes... Ever!
The Funniest Leicester Quotes... Ever!
The Funniest Saints Quotes... Ever!
The Funniest Everton Quotes... Ever!
The Funniest Villa Quotes... Ever!
The Funniest QPR Quotes... Ever!
The Funniest Celtic Quotes... Ever!
The Funniest Rangers Quotes... Ever!

"If they made a film of my life, I think they should get George Clooney to play me."

THE FUNNIEST FOOTBALL QUOTES... EVER!

"Mario woke up this morning with a hardening – in his thigh!"

by Gordon Law

Copyright © 2020 by Eagle Books.

No part of this publication may be reproduced, stored in a retrieval system or transmitted in any form by any means, electronic, mechanical, photocopying, or otherwise, without prior written permission of the publisher Eagle Books.

contact@gmediagroup.co.uk

Printed in Europe and the USA

ISBN: 978-1-917744-21-8
Imprint: Eagle Books

Photos courtesy of: fstockfoto/Shutterstock.com; Ivica Drusany/Shutterstock.com

Contents

Introduction..6

Can You Manage?..9

Talking Balls..19

Call The Manager.......................................31

Say That Again?...39

Game For a Laugh.....................................45

Calling The Shots.......................................63

Off The Pitch..71

Field of Dreams..81

Media Circus..95

Managing Just Fine..................................107

Pundit Paradise..119

Introduction

It might be more than half a century since England were crowned world champions, but when it comes to funny sound bites, the team is among the best on the planet.

Managers and players have helped ease the "many years of hurt" with decades of laughs away from the pitch. There's been an endless array of witty one-liners, foot-in-mouth moments and mixed metaphors from them all.

"I was really surprised when the FA knocked on my doorbell," was one of many bloopers from England forward Michael Owen. A young Wayne Rooney confessed he was "more afraid of my mum than Sven-Goran Eriksson" and an insightful David Beckham once revealed that: "This team has some of the best players in England."

Being England manager is often described as an impossible job and former striker Ian Wright ruled himself out of taking the hot seat: "I've got the passion but no idea of tactics – I'd be like a black Kevin Keegan."

Sven-Goran Eriksson was so nervous about the role he hilariously said: "It's like when you go out with a woman for the first time and you're bound to wonder how it will end up."

There's also been bonkers remarks from Bobby Robson, comic rants from Graham Taylor and gaffes galore from Kevin Keegan.

Many of their classic quips can be found in this unique collection and I hope you laugh as much reading this book as I did in compiling it.

Gordon Law

THE FUNNIEST ENGLAND QUOTES... EVER!

CAN YOU MANAGE?

THE FUNNIEST ENGLAND QUOTES... EVER!

"I certainly wouldn't put money on myself. Working as a national manager is out of the question."

Sven-Goran Eriksson, six days before becoming England boss

"The England job is an impossible job. Particularly for an Englishman, it's tougher than being prime minister."

Glenn Hoddle

"Even the Pope would think twice about taking the England manager's job."

Roy Hodgson – before he took the reins

Can You Manage?

"I was sitting there during the game thinking to myself: 'I can't believe this – I am manager of England'."

Peter Taylor as England caretaker against Italy in 2000

"I'm not interested in the England job, so I hope no one has had a bet on me."

Kevin Keegan a week before he became interim manager

"To be the England manager you must win every game, not do anything in your private life and hopefully not earn too much money."

Sven-Goran Eriksson

THE FUNNIEST ENGLAND QUOTES... EVER!

"I'd have to be living on another planet to believe I was the fans' choice."

Roy Hodgson who got the nod as England boss ahead of Harry Redknapp

"Ninety minutes before a game there's not much a coach can do. You can't talk to players so you sit drinking tea."

Sven-Goran Eriksson

"I used to quite like turnips. Now my wife won't serve them."

Graham Taylor after being called a turnip by the Sun newspaper

Can You Manage?

"I can't stand the cr*p that gets talked by everyone – players, fans, the media, club officials. Why should I waste my time listening to people who are clearly less intelligent than me?"
Fabio Capello

"When Napoleon was asked what he wanted from his generals, he said 'luck'. I don't think Napoleon would have wanted me."
Graham Taylor after defeat to Holland

"I'm thinking of taking a window cleaner's job to fill the spare hour in the evening."
Stuart Pearce on working with England U21s and Manchester City

THE FUNNIEST ENGLAND QUOTES... EVER!

"I'm nervous about meeting so many new people. It's like when you go out with a woman for the first time and you're bound to wonder how it will end up."
Sven-Goran Eriksson before his maiden England game in 2001

"If I am to lose this job they will have to take it away from me."
Kevin Keegan shortly before he resigned

"My advice to the next England manager? Don't lose matches."
Graham Taylor

Can You Manage?

"I feel I have broken the ice with the English people. In 60 days, I have gone from being Volvo Man to Svensational."

Sven-Goran Eriksson

"I've been asked that question for the last six months. It is not fair to expect me to make such a fast decision on something that has been put upon me like that."

Terry Venables on whether he would remain in charge after Euro 96

"I've never eaten anyone so there is no reason anyone should be scared of me."

Fabio Capello

THE FUNNIEST ENGLAND QUOTES... EVER!

"Don Revie was the cleverest of all of us [England managers]. He walked out before they threw him out."
Sven-Goran Eriksson

"It was difficult in the beginning, in the middle and at the end."
Steve McClaren on his time with England

"If the pressure had frightened me, I'd have kept my quality of life at Ipswich, driving my Jag six miles to work every day and getting drunk with the chairman every Saturday night."
Bobby Robson on the England job

Can You Manage?

"Some parts of the job I did very well, but not the key part of getting players to win football matches."
Kevin Keegan

"I've read the book about all the other England managers [The Second Most Important Job in the World]. They were more or less killed, all of them. Why should I be any different?"
Sven-Goran Eriksson

"I don't really know what I'm doing here."
Roy Hodgson in his final press conference having already announced his resignation

THE FUNNIEST ENGLAND QUOTES... EVER!

TALKING BALLS

THE FUNNIEST ENGLAND QUOTES... EVER!

"Playing for England won't faze Carlton [Cole] at all. One of his great attributes is that he doesn't think too much, so I think he'll be OK."
Robert Green

"Sven was top-drawer and I really liked him. He was straight and honest – even if he did look like Mr Burns from The Simpsons."
David James

"The boss said to me, 'If you screw the nut and do what we tell you, then you could play for England'. I did and he was correct."
Jack Charlton on Don Revie

Talking Balls

"Just because I play for England, Walter Winterbottom thinks I understand peripheral vision and positive running."

Jimmy Greaves

"I went back to the room and found Gazza had defecated in my shorts."

John Salako after his England strip had been left in his hotel room for him

"I thought [Glenn Hoddle] said, 'Do you want to visit a brewery?' But it turned out he asked if I'd like to see Eileen Drewery."

Paul Gascoigne on the faith healer

THE FUNNIEST ENGLAND QUOTES... EVER!

"I'm more afraid of my mum than Sven-Goran Eriksson or David Moyes."
Wayne Rooney

"George [Cohen] has hit more photographers than Frank Sinatra."
Bobby Robson on the full-back's crossing

"I met [England No.2] John Gorman during an end-of-season tour in Spain. We were all drinking in a bar and John and I bumped into each other. We had a chat and he told me I'd never play for England unless I grew my hair. I told him to f*ck off."
Julian Dicks

Talking Balls

"Bobby [Robson] told me I could score lots of goals for England and put me on the bench for the first time against Wales. It brought me down to earth 20 minutes from time when he said, 'Get warmed up Garth'."
Gary Lineker

"People think he's some hooligan from up north. He's anything but. He's a gentleman."
Joe Hart on Andy Carroll

"Stan used to put the ball on my centre parting. They don't do that anymore."
Tommy Lawton on Stanley Matthews

THE FUNNIEST ENGLAND QUOTES... EVER!

"We didn't get on. I couldn't warm to the man. He was very egotistical and incredibly arrogant. I think it annoyed him that people compared me to him. He probably thought I was deeply inferior."

Matt Le Tissier on Glenn Hoddle

"He wasn't just cool, he was refrigerated."

Terry Venables on teammate Bobby Moore

"I have to be honest and say that I felt Bobby Robson was a bit bumbling at times. When I first turned up for training, he called me Paul Adams."

Tony Adams

Talking Balls

"We talked Alf [Ramsey] into letting us have a bit of sun [by the hotel pool]. He blew a whistle and we all lay down. Ten minutes later he blew it again and we all turned over."

Jack Charlton on the 1970 World Cup

"I told him in no uncertain terms to go and f*ck himself."

Charlie George to Don Revie after being substituted by the England manager

"What chance has any other top striker got with England while old golden boy Shearer is still on the scene? It's an issue which bugs me."

Andy Cole

THE FUNNIEST ENGLAND QUOTES... EVER!

"With Gazza around, you can expect to get pepper in your dessert and it has been known for him to book a sunbed for one of the black players in the squad."

Dennis Wise on Paul Gascoigne

"Meeting David Beckham... I might take my autograph book!"

David Wheater on his first England call-up

Sir Alf Ramsay: "I'll be watching you for the first 45 minutes and if you don't work harder, I'll pull you off at half-time."

Rodney Marsh: "Blimey – at Manchester City, all we get is an orange and a cup of tea."

Talking Balls

"After six weeks in the England camp, even Jack Charlton could look attractive."

George Cohen

"I knew my England career was not going to get off the mark again when the manager Graham Taylor kept calling me Tony. That's my dad's name."

Mark Hateley

"You look in his eyes and he's 17 – you look at him from behind and he's 32."

David James on Wayne Rooney

THE FUNNIEST ENGLAND QUOTES... EVER!

"Against Brazil [in the 2002 World Cup], he said nothing in the changing room at half-time, absolutely f*ck all, just stood there with a startled look on his face like he, too, believed we were f*cked."

Robbie Fowler on Sven-Goran Eriksson

"We needed Winston Churchill and we got Iain Duncan Smith."

Gareth Southgate gives his verdict on Eriksson's half-time inspiration

"He's obviously really tall."

Michael Owen on his strike partner Peter Crouch

Talking Balls

"Jamie Carragher roomed with me for the England under-21s and he would just eat an apple then throw it in the corner. And he'd wake up in the morning, clear his throat and spit a big greenie onto the wall."

Frank Lampard

Q: "Who is the teacher's pet?"

A: "H Kane – he's always chatting to the gaffer. The skip's always got his ear with the gaffer. He could be plotting... Is that a teacher's pet? I just don't know Harry. I'm not going to give an answer!"

Alex Oxlade-Chamberlain jokes about his teammate

THE FUNNIEST ENGLAND QUOTES... EVER!

CALL THE MANAGER

THE FUNNIEST ENGLAND QUOTES... EVER!

"We didn't underestimate Cameroon. They were just a lot better than we thought."
Bobby Robson

"I'm just saying to your colleague, the referee has got me the sack. Thank him ever so much for that, won't you?"
Graham Taylor to the fourth official after Holland's Ronald Koeman was wrongfully allowed to stay on the pitch

"We need goals when the scoreline is 0-0."
Sven-Goran Eriksson

Call The Manager

"It was nothing personal: if it had been, I would have left him on so he could have suffered like everyone else."

Graham Taylor on the decision to sub Gary Lineker in his last match against Sweden

"At the end of the Argentina game I found myself asking the same question again and again, 'Why am I here?'"

Glenn Hoddle

"Well, we scored nine, and you can't do better than that."

Bobby Robson on hammering Luxembourg

THE FUNNIEST ENGLAND QUOTES... EVER!

"I don't think you can blame a player for missing a penalty. I don't think we missed a penalty individually, I think we missed it collectively."
Stuart Pearce defends his Under-21 side

"It was nearly my finest hour, but life is made up of so nearlies."
Graham Taylor after England threw away a 2-0 lead to draw with Holland

"It wasn't the hand of God, it was the hand of a rascal. God had nothing to do with it."
Bobby Robson

"We have nothing to learn from these people."
Alf Ramsey after a 1970 World Cup defeat to Brazil

"I thought it was like Barack Obama getting the Nobel Peace Prize after eight months as US President."
Fabio Capello on David Beckham winning man of the match for playing half an hour against Belarus

"Do I not like that!?"
Graham Taylor's now-famous reaction after a goal by Poland

THE FUNNIEST ENGLAND QUOTES... EVER!

"What was he doing in the f*cking box? Didn't we tell him to hold the middle of the pitch?"
Graham Taylor after Carlton Palmer's goal against San Marino

"Portugal play football as I like to see it played. As a neutral it was fantastic. Unfortunately I'm not a neutral."
Kevin Keegan after Portugal beat England at Euro 2000

"I never heard a minute's silence like that."
Glenn Hoddle after Princess Diana's death in 1997

Call The Manager

"You're talking about another human being, just watch your language, all right?"
Graham Taylor scolds an England fan for abusing John Barnes

"He crossed nine balls during the game, which was double anyone else on the park."
Steve McClaren on Stewart Downing. Who sent over 4.5 deliveries?

"Except for the two goals, I don't think they had one occasion to score."
Sven-Goran Eriksson after England's 2-2 draw with Austria

THE FUNNIEST ENGLAND QUOTES... EVER!

SAY THAT AGAIN?

THE FUNNIEST ENGLAND QUOTES... EVER!

"If you can't stand the heat in the dressing room, get out of the kitchen."
Terry Venables

"No one wants to commit hari-kari and sell themselves down the river."
Gary Lineker at Euro 92

"Footballers are no different to human beings."
Graham Taylor

"It's about putting square pegs into square holes."
Steve McClaren

Say That Again?

"I was really surprised when the FA knocked on my doorbell."
Michael Owen

"No one's shirt is cast in stone."
Glenn Hoddle

"There is great harmonium in the dressing room."
Sir Alf Ramsey

"Always remember that the goal is at the end of the field, not in the middle."
Sven-Goran Eriksson

THE FUNNIEST ENGLAND QUOTES... EVER!

"With hindsight, it's easy to look at it with hindsight."
Glenn Hoddle

"People want success. It's like coffee, they want it instant."
Bobby Robson

"The defeat wasn't as bad as it sounds on paper."
Steve McClaren

"I am not one to jump over the moon or off a cliff."
Alf Ramsey

Say That Again?

"I'm not so disappointed, just disappointed."
Kevin Keegan

"That's understandable and I understand that."
Terry Venables

"This is like getting to the semi-final of a cup final."
Steve McClaren

"They've done everything that we told them not to do – everything that we told them not to do."
Graham Taylor

THE FUNNIEST ENGLAND QUOTES... EVER!

GAME FOR A LAUGH

THE FUNNIEST ENGLAND QUOTES... EVER!

"The Brazilians were South American, but the Ukrainians will be more European."
Phil Neville

"Watching the Premier League is like Formula One – it's that quick – and then you go to an international game and it's like a game of chess."
Robert Green

"I never hide away from the fact that when Scotland got knocked out of World Cups in the past, like in 1982 and 1986 and 1990, we cheered the roof off, the England team did."
Terry Butcher

Game For a Laugh

"Short back and sides, please."
Ray Parlour in his session with Glenn Hoddle's faith healer Eileen Drewery

"My dad always told me to keep my mouth shut. Now I've realised I've reached the stage where I must learn to do it in big tournaments. I know I'll never be sent off playing for England."
David Beckham before his red card at the 1998 World Cup

"At Wembley it got warmer and warmer as you went up the tunnel and what hit you, apart from the noise, was the smell of fried onions."
Malcolm Macdonald

THE FUNNIEST ENGLAND QUOTES... EVER!

"Maybe I should just go out and kick one of them for old times' sake."

David Beckham ahead of the 2002 World Cup match against Argentina – four years after his infamous red card

"You've got to believe that you're going to win, and I believe we'll win the World Cup until the final whistle blows and we're knocked out."

Peter Shilton

"It's disappointing to be dropped from any team – even my mates' fantasy league team!"

Robert Green sees the funny side after being omitted from the England squad

Game For a Laugh

"I've only taken one penalty before, for Crystal Palace at Ipswich when it was 2-2 in the 89th minute. I hit the post and we went down that year. But I think I would be far more comfortable now than I was then."
Gareth Southgate before his England shoot-out miss at Euro 96

"She [Eileen Drewery] gives the players a shoulder to talk to."
Neil Webb

"Because of the booking I will miss the Holland game – if selected."
Paul Gascoigne

THE FUNNIEST ENGLAND QUOTES... EVER!

"Dennis [Bergkamp] is such a nice man, such a tremendous gentleman with such a lovely family. It's going to be very hard for me to kick him."
Tony Adams before the Holland Euro 96 clash

"The great thing about football captaincy is that when things go wrong, the manager gets the blame."
Gary Lineker

"I'm sure people will always say, 'He's that idiot who missed that penalty'."
Gareth Southgate after his infamous Euro 96 spot kick

Game For a Laugh

"I would walk back from the United States to play for England again."
David Beckham

"107 caps isn't bad for someone who isn't a 'top, top player', is it?"
Steven Gerrard refers to Sir Alex Ferguson's view of the midfielder

"The crowd are shouting, 'England's No.1'. I say No.6, so for the moment I am closer!"
Rob Green jokes about his England snub by having 'England's No.6' stitched on to his gloves

THE FUNNIEST ENGLAND QUOTES... EVER!

"I got a text message from the FA saying I was in the England squad. It was too intellectual for a footballer to have written it. All the spellings and the punctuation were correct."
Curtis Davies

"The Scots believe that if they can just beat England all is well with their football."
Bobby Moore after England give them a 5-0 Hampden beating in 1973

"I will never forget my first game for England at the World Cup. It was against Turkey... No, I mean Tunisia."
David Seaman

Game For a Laugh

"It was nice to get the first session out of the way and get a bit of a feel for each other."
Steven Gerrard gets touchy feely

"To those who say it's a step back, I say b*llocks."
Ian Wright on his call-up at the age of 34

"For Christmas, I'd get Ben Davies some tissues for after when England beat Wales in the Euros."
Dele Alli's banter with his Spurs teammate

"The last time I lifted a weight? Probably that can of Red Bull the other day."
Jamie Vardy

THE FUNNIEST ENGLAND QUOTES... EVER!

"This team has some of the best players in England."
David Beckham

"We did really well in qualifying so I think maybe I'm the problem coming back. They seemed to be fine when I was watching."
Jamie Carragher on England's poor World Cup form

"It was like Deal or No Deal. He had a flipchart and lifted a sheet up to reveal the one with the team on it. I was waiting for the crowd to cheer."
David James on Fabio Capello announcing his team line-up

Game For a Laugh

Brian Clough: "I see you're in the England squad, do you think you're good enough?"
Stuart Pearce: "I'm not sure."
Clough: "I don't, get out!"
Exchange after the defender's first call-up

"Five per cent of me is disappointed [to come second in the group] while the other 50 per cent is just happy that we've qualified."
Michael Owen

"I'd give my right arm to get back into the England team."
Peter Shilton

THE FUNNIEST ENGLAND QUOTES... EVER!

"The first guy I saw was David Beckham. I thought, 'Flipping heck, I've seen this guy on TV with movie stars'."

Darren Bent on arriving at his first England training session

"I wasn't told I was old then – I was told I was cr*p!"

Frank Lampard on playing for England during his 20s

"My half brother is Jamaican, so I might try for them. I have more chance of getting into that squad than England."

Kevin Davies before his solitary cap

Game For a Laugh

"I was in a barbers in Moss Side when my mobile phone rang. This voice said, 'This is Steve McClaren here...'. So I just said, 'Yeah, whatever' and hung up. Then he called again and I listened to his voice and could tell it really was the England manager."

Micah Richards nearly missed his call-up

"I'm certainly not slow, but I'm not the quickest."

Jamie Carragher

"When England play Scotland at anything, even if it's tiddlywinks, they want to win. That's the way it is and always has been."

Mark Hateley

THE FUNNIEST ENGLAND QUOTES... EVER!

"We all want to keep our heads down and do as well as we can. There are times when you can't. We're all human at the end of the day. But it's difficult keeping your head down at six feet seven."
Peter Crouch

"Ray Clemence has got more chance of starting a game for England than me at the moment."
Scott Carson

"As England goalkeeper you are always there to be shot at."
Paul Robinson

Game For a Laugh

"No money in the world can buy a white England shirt."
Alan Shearer

"My heart bleeds for them. Never mind."
Alan Shearer after hearing Scotland had been eliminated at Euro 96

"Don't ever call me a bottler on radio with all those thousands of people listening."
A furious Jamie Carragher after TalkSport presenter Adrian Durham had called him 'a bottler' for withdrawing from England duty

THE FUNNIEST ENGLAND QUOTES... EVER!

"For me what mattered was that we had lost to the Jocks and I have never gone home from Wembley in such a bad mood. I was furious."
Stuart Pearce after a 1-0 defeat to Scotland

"When we were in South Africa, I remember one night I was bored, so me and Wayne Rooney sat in his room and watched his whole wedding on DVD."
Jermain Defoe at the 2010 World Cup

"Have boots won't travel, that's me."
Gordon West on not flying out with England's 1970 World Cup squad

Game For a Laugh

"It's going to be hard for me to make the England team now. I want to play in the 2006 World Cup finals and I may have to seriously consider making myself available for the Republic of Ireland."

The patriotic Zat Knight

"If I had to die on a football pitch, I would want to do it playing for England."

Ian Wright resorts to extreme measures

"The only people who should play for England are English people."

Jack Wilshere

THE FUNNIEST ENGLAND QUOTES... EVER!

CALLING THE SHOTS

THE FUNNIEST ENGLAND QUOTES... EVER!

"Wayne Rooney came into the England set-up as a 17-year-old. He barely said a word because he was so shy. And, when he did, I couldn't understand it because of his strange accent."
Sven-Goran Eriksson on Wayne Rooney

"Michael Owen is a goalscorer – not a natural born one, not yet, that takes time."
Glenn Hoddle at the 1998 World Cup

"The little lad jumped like a salmon and tackled like a ferret."
Sir Bobby Robson on Paul Parker's displays at the 1990 World Cup

Calling The Shots

"Michael Owen is Michael Owen. He has shown it so many times."
Sven-Goran Eriksson

"Young Gareth Barry, you know, he's young."
Kevin Keegan

"Daft as a brush."
Bobby Robson on Paul Gascoigne

"Wayne Rooney is experienced but experienced in what he's been through."
Steve McClaren

THE FUNNIEST ENGLAND QUOTES... EVER!

"I don't like to use the word 'dropped'. He just fell outside the 23."

Roy Hodgson on Ashley Young failing to make the squad

"Talking is silver, but silence is golden."

Sven-Goran Eriksson after David Beckham admitted getting booked to engineer a suspension

"There's a slight doubt about only one player, and that's Tony Adams, who definitely won't be playing tomorrow."

Kevin Keegan

Calling The Shots

"Everybody says Steve McManaman played on the left for me in Euro 96 but he never played on the left. The one time he did play on the left was against Switzerland."

Terry Venables

"I want more from David Beckham. I want him to improve on perfection."

Kevin Keegan

"What can I say about Peter Shilton? Peter Shilton is Peter Shilton and he has been Peter Shilton since the year dot."

Bobby Robson

THE FUNNIEST ENGLAND QUOTES... EVER!

"Kevin Phillips was so keen to join up with England that he almost got here early enough to meet the last squad going home."
Kevin Keegan

"I'm not married to David Beckham – I'm not even engaged to him."
Sven-Goran Eriksson

Bobby Robson: "Good morning, Bobby."
Bryan Robson: "You're Bobby, I'm Bryan!"
The manager greets his midfielder at the team breakfast

Calling The Shots

"When he was dribbling, he used to go through a minefield with his arm, a bit like you go through a supermarket."
Bobby Robson on Paul Gascoigne

"Scholsey, go out there and drop a few hand grenades."
Kevin Keegan to Paul Scholes against Sweden – who was sent off shortly after

"Steve Hodge has been unfit for two weeks, well, no, for 14 days."
Bobby Robson

THE FUNNIEST ENGLAND QUOTES... EVER!

OFF THE PITCH

THE FUNNIEST ENGLAND QUOTES... EVER!

"I don't know if we ate much [of dinner]. But Nancy had not come over for the food."
Sven-Goran Eriksson on the beginning of his relationship with Nancy Dell'Olio

"Jesus was a normal, run-of-the-mill sort of guy who had a genuine gift, just as Eileen [Drewery] has."
Glenn Hoddle

"I used to tell [Nancy Dell'Olio] that she wouldn't have been interested in me had I been a plumber."
Sven-Goran Eriksson

Off The Pitch

Tony Dorigo: "Your tracksuit is disgusting."
David Batty: "It's not mine, it's yours!"
Batty returned to their hotel room, covered in blood and guts from fishing

"I can't read novels. If you have to use your imagination and set the scenes in your own head then you are doing half of the author's work."
David James

"I don't know where they will stay, it's not my concern. I'm hoping there will be a virus."
Fabio Capello when asked about the England WAGs at the 2010 World Cup

THE FUNNIEST ENGLAND QUOTES... EVER!

"We were encouraged to open ourselves to the Japanese cuisine on offer. But having been away from home for so long I could have died for a McDonald's."

Danny Mills on the England squad's 2002 World Cup diet

"I know Sven has a roving eye. He is like a seagull and can wrap his wings around people."

David Davies, executive director of the FA

"I always score one against the Germans."

Gary Lineker after being bowled out for one run, batting for MCC v Germany at Lord's

Off The Pitch

"You won't be surprised to know that I have some faith in astrologers and particularly what the stars predict for Scorpios."
Glenn Hoddle

"I don't see how one kebab can be the difference between beating one or three men or running from box to box or scoring a goal."
Paul Gascoigne is confused about being left out of England's World Cup squad

"I drink tea every morning and in the afternoon. It's very nice! EastEnders? No I don't watch that... but I'm sure it's very good."
Sven-Goran Eriksson

THE FUNNIEST ENGLAND QUOTES... EVER!

"I could not believe what was happening to me. He was a master in the art of love-making. He did not use a condom. There was no contraception. He was not concerned about me getting pregnant."
Faria Alam, ex-FA secretary on her fling with Sven-Goran Eriksson

"We had a wonderful dinner. When we finished I was full of anticipation – but he wanted to clear the plates away first."
Faria Alam

"Sven is a very giving man in the area of passion."
Faria Alam

Off The Pitch

"It's part and parcel of being a footballer these days. I think a few of the lads would have liked to have seen a couple of them [the paparazzi] eaten by the lions."

Joe Cole on the photographers who followed him and his England teammates during a safari trip in South Africa

"I only went in for a filling and I came out drunk – it must have been some anaesthetic! But get the video tapes of that tournament and you'll see how successful the dentist's chair was!"

Paul Gascoigne, recalling an infamous squad drinking session prior to Euro 96

THE FUNNIEST ENGLAND QUOTES... EVER!

"I feel sorry for Nancy – not only does she look like a drag queen but she's latched on to someone who clearly doesn't love her."
Faria Alam on Sven-Goran Eriksson's former partner Nancy Dell'Olio

"Yesterday evening they drank beer, before the game. You can ask them! It's true, I changed something. Used my imagination. It was free. South African beer."
Fabio Capello, the strict disciplinarian

"In Sweden we don't discuss our private lives. We have other things to talk about."
Tord Grip, Sven-Goran Eriksson's No.2

Off The Pitch

"Four hours after playing for England against World Cup finalists West Germany in front of 68,000 at Wembley, I was attempting to clean a sheepdog's diarrhoea from a shagpile carpet at my home."
David Armstrong

"The Gulf War was a cakewalk compared with Eriksson's love life."
FA head of communications Paul Newman and former BBC war correspondent

"I married a girl who was very easily told, 'If you marry me, you're marrying football'."
Graham Taylor

THE FUNNIEST ENGLAND QUOTES... EVER!

FIELD OF DREAMS

THE FUNNIEST ENGLAND QUOTES... EVER!

"Denis Law kicked me, right in front of the Queen and I've still got the scar. It was worth it, though. England 9, Scotland 3."

Bobby Robson on the 1961 clash

"At least his hair is OK."

David James after David Beckham, sporting a cornrows hairstyle, suffers a hand injury against South Africa

"The Brazilians were shocked, and I supposed that's why they didn't tackle me, because they thought there was no way an Englishman is going to do this."

John Barnes on his fine goal against Brazil

Field of Dreams

"I played so badly that even my parents booed me off when I was substituted."
Theo Walcott for England U21s

"The reason we went out of Euro 2000 wasn't anything to do with what happened in the last minute against Romania."
Gary Neville – are you sure?

"As Gazza got up, he asked [Andy] Goram why he had bothered diving to try and save it! Then he said, 'Where's Hendry? Has he gone to get me a pie?'."
Teddy Sheringham after Paul Gascoigne's strike against Scotland at Euro 96

THE FUNNIEST ENGLAND QUOTES... EVER!

"It was like asking Frank Sinatra to sing in front of three-dozen people."

Jimmy Greaves describes playing in front of small crowds for England at the 1962 World Cup

"He might as well have caught the ball, put it under his shirt and run home with it."

Rio Ferdinand on having a penalty appeal denied against Montenegro

"Don't ask me about VAR. I don't know what it stands for."

Jamie Vardy after his England goal was cancelled out

Field of Dreams

"At the time it was really special, especially against the old enemy. In Scotland they try to erase the game from the memory. If you tried to talk about it they'd change the subject."
Jimmy Armfield on England's 9-3 victory

"When Incey was running around with his head bandaged [against Italy], he looked like a pint of Guinness."
Paul Gascoigne

"It would have been great to win 1-0. But 0-0 seems even better because it shows character to get such a result."
David Beckham after a stalemate in Turkey

THE FUNNIEST ENGLAND QUOTES... EVER!

"As I was heading towards goal, Alan Ball was shouting: 'Hursty, Hursty give me the ball!' I said to myself: 'Sod you Bally, I'm on a hat-trick'."
Geoff Hurst recalling his memorable third goal in the 1966 World Cup final

"I didn't watch the England v Argentina match in 1998. I can't remember why not. It may have been past my bedtime."
Theo Walcott

"It was really difficult for us playing in the midday sun with that three o'clock kick-off."
David Beckham after a win over Paraguay at the 2006 World Cup

Field of Dreams

"It was a sense of numbness really – how the hell are we out of this World Cup? It even got to the point where there were weird ideas – maybe if we'd had brown rice rather than white."

Rio Ferdinand clutches at straws following England's 2006 World Cup exit

"'Wait until you come to Turkey!' was the shout with fingers being passed across the throat. And that was just the kit man."

Gareth Southgate after beating the Turks

"If you want to have a great party at Wembley, don't invite the Germans."

Alan Shearer on England's Euro 96 defeat

THE FUNNIEST ENGLAND QUOTES... EVER!

"We could have scored a second at any time but used our experience to play out a 1-0 victory."

Phil Neville after England's win against Macedonia

"I thought, 'That's a sweet connection, I never felt it touch my foot'. Then I looked around and it's in the back of the net."

Paul Robinson on his mis-kick from a back pass which resulted in an own goal

"She said, 'Why didn't you belt it?'"

Gareth Southgate on what his mum said after his Euro 96 penalty miss

Field of Dreams

"When I scored my first goal for England, I was so excited I didn't know what to do or where to run. David [Beckham] just pointed and said, 'Well the England fans are that way, mate'."
Wayne Rooney gets a helping hand

"That save from Pele's header was the best I ever made. I didn't have any idea how famous it would become – to start with, I didn't even realise I'd made it at all."
Gordon Banks

"It was like playing people from outer space."
Syd Owen after England's 6-3 defeat to Hungary in 1953

THE FUNNIEST ENGLAND QUOTES... EVER!

"I am sure some people think I have not got the brains to be that clever – but I do have the brains."

David Beckham on claims he deliberately got booked against Wales

"Nice to see your own fans booing you. That's what loyal support is."

Wayne Rooney blasts the England fans for jeering a 0-0 draw against Algeria

"When the final whistle went I was in shock. The next thing I knew I was on the floor with Nobby Stiles giving me a big, toothless kiss."

George Cohen on the World Cup win

Field of Dreams

"I sort of fell to the ground and relaxed for a second and it just went 'boom'. It was like, 'Oh my god', but it was like everywhere. There's a bit, if you ever see the footage, where Gary Stevens comes over and asks what's wrong. And I go, 'I've sh*t myself'. I just didn't know what to do. Thank God I had dark blue shorts on that day. I'm shovelling it out and rubbing myself on the grass like a dog. It was amazing how much space I found after that though, I was stinking."

Gary Lineker on the time he pooed himself against Ireland at Italia 90

"I'm on top of the moon."

Lee Hendrie after his England debut

THE FUNNIEST ENGLAND QUOTES... EVER!

"Football is a simple game where 22 men chase a ball for 90 minutes and at the end, the Germans win."

Gary Lineker on West Germany's penalty shoot-out triumph in 1990

"I haven't seen [Ronaldinho's] winner yet. It's not that I'm avoiding it, just that my little girl has been watching Teletubbies all the time."

David Seaman on the chipped free-kick that sent England out of the World Cup

"I was hit by an apple but, apart from that, I didn't experience any problems."

David James after the Turkey clash

Field of Dreams

"It didn't bother me when the Hampden hordes chanted, 'Bobby Moore, superstar, walks like a woman and he wears a bra'. This should keep them quiet for a bit."
Bobby Moore after winning his 100th cap in a 5-0 win over Scotland in 1973

"He was screaming like a girl... and you can tell him that as well."
Steven Gerrard recalls a tackle on Didi Hamann at Euro 2000

"We're like 11 bulldogs who'll never give up and basically die on the pitch."
Ashley Cole at Euro 2012

THE FUNNIEST ENGLAND QUOTES... EVER!

MEDIA CIRCUS

THE FUNNIEST ENGLAND QUOTES... EVER!

Q: "How would you like to leave the England job?"

Sven-Goran Eriksson: "Alive."

The manager in a 2006 TV interview

"Gary Neville is petrified of you lot. He's young, he's reading the papers and he's coming up to me every two minutes asking, 'Have you seen what they're saying?'"

Terry Venables

"You can call me a turnip, but don't ever call me Gordon."

Graham Taylor

Media Circus

"Absolute f*cking b*llocks. Don't give me that one. Two shots on target? What about all the ones they threw themselves in front of. Don't hit me with statistics. When we had that much possession and you talk about two shots on target?"

Roy Hodgson to reporters after England's narrow win over Norway

"To appease the people writing about me, I'd have to play 23 players against Yugoslavia next month. And I don't think the regulations allow that."

Bobby Robson

THE FUNNIEST ENGLAND QUOTES... EVER!

"I swear all the time. I swear in front of my wife. I never used to when I was a kid but I do now, so there you go. It's 2014. People swear – and I swear."

Roy Hodgson responds to the media who criticised him for swearing at a press conference after a win over Norway

"As it was the media who tipped us to win, I thought one or two of their jobs might be in jeopardy. Not likely – it was me they were after."

Bobby Robson on England's poor Euro 88 campaign

Media Circus

"Hitler didn't tell us when he was going to send over those doodlebugs, did he?"

Bobby Robson on refusing to name his team before a World Cup qualifier against Sweden

"You won't see me in 20 or 30 years' time, sitting and slagging off an England performance. Shoot me if you do."

Frank Lampard on the TV pundits who slammed the team at the 2006 World Cup

"I'm not prepared to make any comments on the World Cup in Qatar in 1922."

Roy Hodgson

THE FUNNIEST ENGLAND QUOTES... EVER!

"I will not let these people get to me or rattle me. They have no qualifications. They have never been anywhere or done anything in football. Why should I listen to them?"
Bobby Robson on the media

"We will prove an awful lot of people wrong – especially that bloke at the back today."
Steven Gerrard is irked by a French journo, who questioned England's ability

Journalist: "What do you admire about Germany?"
Terry Venables: "Their results."
After the Euro 96 penalty shoot-out defeat

Media Circus

Graham Taylor: "Listen Rob, I cannot have faces like yours around me. I can't Rob. I'll tell you this now, if you were one of my players with a face like that, I'd f*cking kick you out, you would never have a chance. Get yourself up man, put a smile on your face, get ready for business. Come on Rob, let's have a little of it back at you. Come on, a bit more of a smile Rob. F*cking hell. The whole nation rests on whether Rob Shepherd is happy or not."

Journalist Rob Shepherd: "I hope I'm smiling tomorrow, I really do. But I just worry."

Graham Taylor: "Listen. You worry, Rob. You worry. But don't make the f*cking rest of us worry, Rob! Go and worry on your own!"

Exchange at the pre-Holland press briefing during England's 1994 World Cup campaign

THE FUNNIEST ENGLAND QUOTES... EVER!

"I have to make a living just like you. I happen to make mine in a nice way. You make yours in a nasty way."

Sir Alf Ramsey to reporters

Sven-Goran Eriksson: "I will not tell Neville to kick Reyes."

Reporter: "You won't have to."

Exchange at a press conference before England v Spain

"The English press are a very nice bunch of b*stards."

Graham Taylor

Media Circus

"Oh misery, misery, what's going to become of me?"

Graham Taylor quotes Buddy Holly to the press after England's 2-2 draw with Holland

"Hi, this is Jamie Vardy from Vardy News – what is the diameter of your head?"

Jamie Vardy gate-crashes one of Harry Maguire's England interviews

"What does that says about the rest of us? Are we all cr*p then?"

Steven Gerrard to a reporter who claimed England might struggle if Wayne Rooney misses the World Cup

THE FUNNIEST ENGLAND QUOTES... EVER!

"You're all such nice people. Sometimes I wonder who writes all the articles."
Sven-Goran Eriksson to reporters

Scottish journalist: "Welcome to Scotland, Sir Alf."
Sir Alf Ramsey: "You must be f*cking joking."
When England faced the Scots in 1968

"Gentlemen, if you want to write whatever you want to write, you can write it because that is all I am going to say."
Steve McClaren before leaving the press conference after a win over Andorra

Media Circus

Interviewer: "What do you think of England's training facilities?"

Gareth Southgate: "It's hardly Club Tropicana."

Interviewer: "Who do you think will make the team?"

Southgate: "You won't be getting any Careless Whispers from me."

The defender gets Wham/George Michael songs into his interview at the 1998 World Cup

"It's a vicious circle. Once the bandwagon starts rolling it's a snowball effect. Obviously you've got to take it with a pinch of salt."

Michael Owen responds to media criticism of David James in full cliche mode

THE FUNNIEST ENGLAND QUOTES... EVER!

MANAGING JUST FINE

THE FUNNIEST ENGLAND QUOTES... EVER!

"The letters I get tend to start with things like, 'Dear Stupid' or 'Dear Big Head'. One began, 'Dear Alfie boy'."
Sir Alf Ramsey

"My grandmother never understood you could be paid so much for kicking a ball. So every time I see her, she slips me £5 or £10."
Sven-Goran Eriksson

"I think everyone in the stadium went home happy, except all those people in Romania."
Ron Greenwood after a World Cup qualifier in Romania

Managing Just Fine

"Against France we'll have to be at our best both technically, tactically and spirit-wise."
Kevin Keegan

"Playing with wingers is more effective against European sides like Brazil than English sides like Wales."
Ron Greenwood

"Compared to the preparation Brazil have had, we are motorways behind them, absolute motorways. Still, it's no use crying over spilt milk, we'll just have to get a new cow."
Glenn Hoddle

THE FUNNIEST ENGLAND QUOTES... EVER!

"When you talk as much as he does none of it can mean very much."

Ron Greenwood on Scotland rival Ally MacLeod

"Normally, if I see Sweden in any competition, I want them to win, but this time, no. We have to kill them. We have to kill Sweden."

Sven-Goran Eriksson

"My biggest mistake of the World Cup was not taking Eileen Drewery."

Glenn Hoddle after England were knocked out of the 1998 tournament

Managing Just Fine

"Look at the Irish. They sing their national anthem and none of them know the words. Jack [Charlton] sings, and all he knows is 'Cushy Butterfield' and 'Blaydon Races'. But look at the pride they have in those green shirts."
England No.2 Lawrie McMenemy

"Argentina are the second best team in the world, and there's no higher praise than that."
Kevin Keegan

"England have to play like England. But maybe a little bit better."
Franco Baldini, Fabio Capello's assistant

THE FUNNIEST ENGLAND QUOTES... EVER!

"I'm not thinking about what happened in the past. In life, you never know. A warrior could come and kick you in the street tomorrow."
Sven-Goran Eriksson

"I'm glad it is not Ukraine because I'm not your man for a 0-0 in Kiev."
Kevin Keegan after England were paired with Scotland in the play-offs for Euro 2000

"I'm beginning to wonder what the national vegetable of Norway is."
Graham Taylor after being compared to a turnip and onion after England's games with Sweden and Spain

Managing Just Fine

"You don't win a game by talking, you win a game by playing."
Roy Hodgson

"Everyone in the men's side is delighted and we hope they go all the way."
Steve McClaren sends his congratulations to the England women's team on qualifying for the World Cup. Ooo er!

"The Germans only have one player under 22 and he's 23."
Kevin Keegan on England's Euro 2000 opponents

THE FUNNIEST ENGLAND QUOTES... EVER!

"I suppose I'll have to get used to being called 'Sir' but if a player gets formal on the field I will clobber them."

Sir Alf Ramsey on his knighthood in 1967

"Eighteen months ago, Sweden were arguably one of the best three teams in Europe and that would include Germany, Holland, Russia and anybody else if you like."

Bobby Robson

"Make sure your shirts are tucked in and you've all been to the toilet."

Howard Wilkinson's final words to his England players before a match with Finland

Managing Just Fine

"I'm not a moralist or saying that you have to go to church on a Sunday to captain England."
Sven-Goran Eriksson defends giving Michael Owen the arm band

"England have the best fans in the world and Scotland's are second to none."
Kevin Keegan

"I used to have my elbows up in the air protecting my face, which is why I am still very pretty."
England U21 boss Stuart Pearce offers words of advice to Craig Dawson who took a nasty blow to the head against Norway

THE FUNNIEST ENGLAND QUOTES... EVER!

"I'm happy with my language progress – the only difficulty when I tour Premier League matches is that different people talk to me in different accents – and sometimes I can hardly understand a word."
England boss Fabio Capello reflects on a visit to Anfield

"There was an in-built desire to beat Scotland when I was growing up."
Glenn Hoddle

"Argentina won't be at Euro 2000 because they're from South America."
Kevin Keegan

Managing Just Fine

"I said right at the start I would live and die by results and results haven't gone my way. In that sense we have failed."

Steve McClaren chooses his words very carefully

"I'm a firm believer that if the other side scores first you have to score twice to win."

FA technical director Howard Wilkinson

"Our best football will come against the right type of opposition. A team who come to play football and not act as animals."

Sir Alf Ramsey on a physical Argentina in the 1966 World Cup quarter-final

THE FUNNIEST ENGLAND QUOTES... EVER!

PUNDIT PARADISE

THE FUNNIEST ENGLAND QUOTES... EVER!

"It's not what I'd call a must-win game, but it's a game England have to win."
Graham Taylor at Euro 2012

"I've got the passion but no idea of tactics – I'd be like a black Kevin Keegan."
Ian Wright

"There's Cassano, powering one into Ashley Cole's backside."
BBC commentator Guy Mowbray

"If Walcott scores it's a different kettle of story."
Adrian Chiles on Ukraine v England

Pundit Paradise

"England are learning to walk before they can run, with their feet nailed firmly on the ground."
Clive Tyldesley

"Steven Gerrard is not the kind of guy who rattles feathers."
Tony Cascarino at Euro 2012

"Seaman's jersey seems to have all the colours of the rainbow in it – yellow, red, green, black."
Alan Green

"England were beaten in the sense that they lost."
Dickie Davis

THE FUNNIEST ENGLAND QUOTES... EVER!

"There could be fatalities – or, even worse, injuries."
Phil Neal on England's trip to Turkey

"I can see England winning tonight, but I can also see them losing."
Lee Dixon

"England are being numerically outnumbered in midfield."
Mark Lawrenson

"England now have three fresh men with three fresh legs."
Jimmy Hill

Pundit Paradise

"I think this could be our best victory over Germany since the war."
John Motson on England's 5-1 success

"You've been sh*te, son, in your daft pink boots."
Richard Keys on Theo Walcott, unaware his mic was still on

"Shearer could be at 100 per cent fitness but not peak fitness."
Graham Taylor

"England should literally put Algeria to bed."
Andy Townsend

THE FUNNIEST ENGLAND QUOTES... EVER!

"I'm not saying we shouldn't have a foreign manager, but I think he should definitely be English."
Paul Merson

"That's football – Northern Ireland have had several chances and not scored. England have had no chances and scored twice."
Trevor Brooking

Des O'Connor: "If England win the World Cup, will you come back and sing a duet with me?"
Elton John: "If they win, I'll come back and sleep with you."

Pundit Paradise

ITV's Mark Pougatch: "What is Ross Barkley's best position?"

Roy Keane: "Probably on the bench."

"There've been a countless number of corners. A round dozen we make it, which I suppose means we can count them."
Barry Davies during England v Albania

Mike Channon: "We've got to get bodies in the box. The French do it, the Italians do it, the Brazilians do it."

Brian Clough: "Even educated bees do it."

The ITV World Cup pundits in 1986

THE FUNNIEST ENGLAND QUOTES... EVER!

"The World Cup is every four years so it's going to be a perennial problem."
Gary Lineker

"The man's like a wet fish. He's got as much passion as a tadpole."
Ian Wright on Sven-Goran Eriksson

"If Glenn Hoddle were any other nationality, he would have had 70 or 80 caps for England."
John Barnes

"Adams is stretching himself, looking for Seaman."
Brian Moore

Pundit Paradise

"His return gives England another key to its bow."
Stuart Pearce

"The midfield picks itself: Beckham, Scholes, Gerrard and AN Other."
Phil Neal

"Steven Gerrard makes runs into the box better than anyone. So does Frank Lampard."
Jamie Redknapp

"If England are going to win this match, they're going to have to score a goal."
Jimmy Hill

THE FUNNIEST ENGLAND QUOTES... EVER!

"The one thing England have got is spirit, resolve, grit and determination."

Alan Hansen

"He looks just like his mum has told him to come in for tea."

Gareth Southgate on Wayne Rooney being subbed at the 2006 World Cup

"It was a toughicult match for Upson to come into."

Alan Shearer at the 2010 World Cup

"Crouch is absolutely centrifugal to Sven's plans."

Mike Parry

Pundit Paradise

"Someone in the England team will have to grab the ball by the horns."
Ron Atkinson

"We're taking 22 players to Italy, sorry, to Spain... where are we, Jim?"
Bobby Robson on the 1998 World Cup

"Without being too harsh on David, he cost us the match."
Ian Wright on England's World Cup exit

"Too many players looked like fish on trees."
Paul Merson on England's defeat to Croatia

THE FUNNIEST ENGLAND QUOTES... EVER!

"I wouldn't back England to beat a team of nuns 9-0."
Brian Clough before the Liechtenstein game

"He looks as if he's been playing for England all his international career."
Trevor Brooking

"For England, it's as if the genie's in the bottle and they haven't got a bottle opener."
George Hamilton

"Just look at the results that he hasn't produced."
Bobby Gould on Steve McClaren

Pundit Paradise

"Poland nil, England nil, though England are now looking the better value for their nil."
Barry Davies

"Mabbutt has now played seven consecutive games for England, this is his seventh."
Martin Tyler

"Steve McClaren will have a pair of sharp, canny shoulders to listen to."
David Platt

"Retiring will put years on his career."
Don Howe on Paul Scholes

THE FUNNIEST ENGLAND QUOTES... EVER!

www.ingramcontent.com/pod-product-compliance
Lightning Source LLC
Chambersburg PA
CBHW050253120526
44590CB00016B/2326